A very tiny baby bug
fell into a china jug.

An ant was in there, eating jam.

'Hello,' he said. 'My name is Sam.'

‘Please help me out,’ said Baby Bug.

So Sam got out and gave a tug.

Then Baby Bug and little Sam,
fell off the jug on to the ham.

‘I love ham,’ said Baby Bug.
‘Yum, yum, yum!’ And in she dug.
But …

Look out! Look out! Here comes Pam!

Look out! Look out! Wham, bam, slam!

‘Quick, let's hide,’ said Baby Bug.

And she and Sam hid in the mug.

Lucky Sam and Baby Bug.
This hiding place was safe and snug.